An Inevitability of Emerging Youth

An Inevitability of Emerging Youth

~

Marybeth Adler

Advise the Heart

Contents

should not be considered a substitute for professional advice. The reader is encouraged to seek the advice of qualified professionals, such as licensed psychologists, counselors, or healthcare providers, regarding specific issues related to the well-being and development of adolescent children.

The author and publishers make no representations or warranties of any kind, express or implied, about the completeness, accuracy, reliability, suitability, or availability of the information contained in this book. Any reliance the reader places on such information is strictly at their own risk.

The author and publishers disclaim any responsibility for any loss, injury, claim, liability, or damage of any kind resulting from, arising out of, or in any way related to the use or misuse of the information presented in this book. This includes but is not limited to, any actions taken by parents or guardians based on the content of the book.

The book addresses sensitive topics related to adolescent development, including sexual urges, and it is the responsibility of the reader to exercise discretion and judgment in applying the information to their specific circumstances. The book is not a replacement for open communication with children, professional advice, or appropriate medical guidance.

By reading this book, the reader acknowledges and agrees to the terms of this legal disclaimer. If the reader does not agree with these terms, they should not use or rely on the information provided in "An Inevitability of Emerging Youth."

First Printing, 2024

ISBN: 979-8-8690-8414-9
EISBN: 979-8-8690-8415-6

1

∽

An Introduction

Undoubtedly, the most pivotal phase in a person's journey unfolds during the eight to ten years leading up to their twenty-first birthday. Within this timeframe, the forces of Heredity, a paramount developmental factor, yield their outcomes, and the seeds sown before birth and during childhood come to fruition. Simultaneously, the second influential factor, Environment, takes center stage, shaping the still malleable nature through circumstances. The interplay of these two forces leaves an indelible mark on the resulting individual's character.

This transformative period is commonly referred to in two significant phases: (1) Puberty, and (2) Adolescence. Puberty marks the emergence of developed reproductive organs, with the once neutral child assuming the distinctive traits of man or woman. The onset of puberty varies among individuals, occurring between the ages of eleven to sixteen. While the changes during this period may not be abrupt, they unfold at a relatively rapid pace.

Adolescence, on the other hand, denotes the phase where the individual approaches the adult archetype, having already undergone puberty. This period spans the latter half of the developmental journey and may extend up to the age of twenty-five. Far from being a fleeting stage, adolescence encompasses a more extended timeline, characterized by a continuing process of growth and self-discovery.

Understanding the intricacies of this critical period is essential for both individuals experiencing it and those guiding them through it. The nuanced dynamics of Heredity and Environment play a crucial role in shaping the trajectory of this journey, making it imperative for society to foster environments that nurture and support the positive development of emerging youth. Embracing the complexity of these formative years is key to cultivating a holistic and empathetic approach to the challenges and opportunities inherent in the path to adulthood.

2

❧

Blossoming Flowers - Emerging Young Adults

Exploration of Physical Transformations

In this pivotal period of life, characterized by the eight to ten years leading up to the twenty-first birthday, a profound metamorphosis occurs within the girl's bodily framework. The skeleton undergoes not only substantial growth but also marked alterations and development. Particularly noticeable changes manifest in the shape and inclination of the pelvis, a central element in the female anatomy.

During childhood, the female pelvis bears a resemblance to its male counterpart. However, with the onset of puberty, the vertical portion of the hip bones undergoes expansion and a change in shape. The brim of the pelvis transforms from a more heart-shaped form to a wide oval, significantly increasing the pelvic girdle's width. This intricate evolution contributes to the distinctive gait and running style observed in adult women.

Simultaneously, the angle formed by the spinal column's junction with the back of the pelvis, known as the sacro-vertebral angle, becomes more pronounced. This, in conjunction with the growth and development of internal organs specific to women, shapes the characteristic female pelvic structure. Notably, these differences between male and female pelves become prominently evident during puberty, and their rapid development ensures unmistakable distinctions between a properly developed girl of sixteen or eighteen years and a boy.

The growth and development of muscles accompanying the bony framework play a crucial role. In some instances, muscles may outgrow bones, leading to a distinct lankiness and slackness of figure. Alternatively, the rapid growth of bones may outpace muscle development, resulting in a phenomenon known as "growing pain."

The remarkable changes extend beyond the skeletal system to encompass other physical features. The bust undergoes rapid development, contributing not only to the girl's physical appearance but also preparing for the maternal role of nurturing infants. Concurrently, the hands and feet do not grow in proportion with limbs, showcasing a more aesthetically pleasing contrast with the fully developed limbs.

Within the internal organs, the pelvis assumes particular importance. The uterus, or womb, expands significantly, preparing to safeguard the developing child until it can sustain an independent existence. Similarly, the ovaries, responsible for producing ovules or eggs, experience growth in both size and structure.

It is crucial to recognize that the years following puberty are characterized not only by rapid physiological changes but also by the potential for irreparable damage. Vigilance and understanding are paramount for those overseeing young girls to navigate these challenges, ensuring their well-being during this transformative phase.

Mental and Emotional Evolution

The metamorphosis during adolescence extends beyond the physical realm, encompassing profound changes in mental and emotional dimensions. While there may be a slight reduction in the ability to memorize, faculties such as attention, reasoning, and imagination experience rapid development. This period is marked by the emergence of an appreciation for beauty, particularly in landscapes, a facet often dormant during childhood.

The adolescent undergoes a comprehensive evolution in outlook, self-perception, and interactions with others. The rapid changes in reproductive organs find parallels in mental and moral spheres, introducing new, often misunderstood sensations —feelings of unrest, vague desires, and heightened self-awareness, replacing the unconscious egoism of childhood.

Analogous to the natural processes witnessed during spring, the adolescent experiences a profound transformation, transitioning from a bare and dry winter state to the vibrant beauty of spring. Unfortunately, this remarkable journey is often overlooked due to its common occurrence. The challenge lies in bridging the generational gap, understanding the depth of adolescent experiences, and fostering an empathetic environment.

Navigating the uncharted territories of adolescence requires a nuanced understanding of the challenges faced by young individuals. The instability of both physical and mental aspects demands careful consideration. While the physical changes may manifest as lateral curvature of the spine, mental shifts involve rapid alterations in friendships, romantic interests, and heroes.

Social Dynamics: Gang Spirit and Gregariousness

The adolescent experience is not confined to

individual transformation but extends to social dynamics. Adolescents, both boys and girls, form groups (or gangs, squads, cliques) characterized by high levels of organization. These groups create their languages, shorthand, passwords, and even rituals. The phenomenon of gregariousness, or the "gang spirit," provides insights into the future capacity to organize individuals into collective endeavors.

Understanding and redirecting this natural inclination toward organized social behavior can yield positive outcomes. It serves as the foundation for future abilities to collaborate and achieve common goals—an essential skill in public and national spheres, where individual efforts may fall short.

Spiritual and Religious Evolution

Religious fervor and earnest conviction mark the adolescent's approach to spirituality. The phenomenon of "conversion" frequently occurs during this phase, leading the individual to perceive eternal truths from a refreshed perspective. The post-conversion period is often characterized by intense love, devotion, and a desire to prove oneself worthy.

However, this fervor can give way to intellectual doubt and spiritual darkness, mirroring the cyclical nature of adolescent experiences. The ability to withstand and emerge from this period of doubt shapes the individual's religious conviction and devotion in adulthood.

The circumstances and influences surrounding the adolescent significantly impact their religious journey. Hero-worship and the inclination to emulate parents, guardians, or teachers play a crucial role. The ideals formed during adolescence often persist into adulthood, emphasizing the importance of positive role models and supportive environments.

Challenges and Opportunities

As adolescents grapple with physical, mental, and emotional changes, they encounter challenges that demand understanding and intelligent sympathy from their caregivers. The dawn of the sexual instinct, often arising without full comprehension, adds another layer of complexity. The differences in experiences between sheltered and unsheltered environments underscore the need for guidance and support.

Parents, as primary influencers, bear the responsibility of instilling habits of self-control, discipline, and obedience from an early age. The choices made during childhood reverberate into adolescence, impacting the individual's ability to navigate challenges effectively. The interplay of heredity and environment underscores the importance of fostering positive influences to ensure the well-rounded development of adolescents.

In conclusion, the adolescent journey is a multifaceted exploration of physical, mental, and emotional dimensions. It demands a nuanced understanding, compassion, and proactive guidance from caregivers and society at large. Recognizing the unique challenges and opportunities presented during this transformative phase is paramount to nurturing the next generation into responsible, fulfilled individuals.

3

∿

Obligations as Parents of Girls

In navigating the multifaceted landscape of contemporary adolescence, addressing the nuanced needs of young girls involves a comprehensive exploration of our societal obligations. A mere proclamation of duty is insufficient; we must embark on an extensive journey to illuminate the path forward, considering every facet of their existence.

Initiating our inquiry into the physical well-being of adolescent girls, we find that their elemental necessities align with the broader requirements of all living beings: sustenance, warmth, shelter, exercise, and rest, with an added layer of care during periods of illness.

Dietary considerations remain a critical linchpin. Despite the strides made in nutritional science, educational institutions, particularly prestigious schools, may yet falter in providing adequate emphasis on proper dietetics for children and adolescents. A comprehensive reassessment is in order. The integration of a substantial quantity of milk into daily diets is advocated, with the suggestion to commence each day with wholesome options such as porridge and milk or other cereal preparations.

In the realm of meals, a judicious and balanced approach is indispensable. The midday repast should encompass a diverse array of fresh meats, fish, or poultry, accompanied by a profusion of green vegetables and a liberal serving of a delectable sweet pudding. Notably, our dietary catalogues often fall short in supplying sufficient quantities of milk, butter, and sugar. There exists an unfounded bias against sugar, which recent research has debunked, establishing it as a valuable muscle food when consumed judiciously.

The temporal cadence and regularity of meals emerge as paramount considerations. Snacking between meals, a commonplace practice during childhood and adolescence, can perturb digestion and sow the seeds for unhealthy cravings. Such dietary habits may even pave the way for issues such as alcohol cravings in later years. Therefore, instating a regimen of regular, nutritious meals devoid of intermittent snacking assumes foundational importance.

Transitioning to the topic of warmth, it emerges as a critical factor in overall health and development. Appropriate clothing, woven from wool or equivalent alternatives, plays a pivotal role in maintaining optimal temperature. However, it is observed that adolescents, particularly girls, might occasionally prioritize clothing for its aesthetic allure rather than its primary function. This proclivity towards fashionable yet uncomfortable clothing, exemplified by tight waists and high-heeled shoes, calls for a nuanced intervention. Encouraging a refined and artistic taste in clothing choices can potentially mitigate these tendencies.

Sleep, as an indispensable pillar of well-being, demands our attention. Adolescents frequently fall short of the recommended duration of sleep, impacting both physical and mental health. The creation of an environment conducive to quality sleep is non-negotiable. Adequate bedding, access to fresh air, and a comfortable sleeping space contribute significantly to the rejuvenating nature of sleep.

The specter of overcrowded living spaces also looms large, directly impacting the quality of sleep. The scarcity of suitable dwellings compels families into confined spaces, often sharing beds. While our understanding of ventilation has progressed, the advocacy for open windows remains a crucial aspect of fostering a healthy living environment.

Shifting focus to exercise, adolescence emerges as a pivotal period where physical activity, including athletics, games, and dancing, takes on heightened significance. Team sports, in particular, not only foster physical health but also impart valuable life skills such as teamwork, discipline, loyalty, and co-operation. The import of instilling the right spirit in which games should be played cannot be overstated, as it profoundly shapes the character of individuals.

Regrettably, gymnastics lags in popularity and accessibility. Systematized exercises, crucial for overall physical and moral development, find inadequate representation in elementary schools due to a lack of well-equipped gymnasia and trained instructors. Stressing the importance of gymnastics not only as a physical exercise but as a means to instill discipline, cooperation, and loyalty is paramount.

Swimming, an ostensibly inexpensive and beneficial exercise, regrettably finds itself relegated to the shadows. Public baths, despite their existence, are insufficient, limiting access for school children. Rectifying this imbalance necessitates a fundamental reevaluation of our national education system, aligning it with the initial ideal of doing the best for our young people in body, soul, and spirit. Our responsibilities extend beyond the mere academic realm; they encompass fostering an environment that nurtures physical health, emotional well-being, and the development of robust character traits in our adolescent girls.

In conclusion, our duty transcends the superficial acknowledgment of responsibilities. It delves into the intricate tapestry of adolescent needs, urging a meticulous examination and an earnest commitment to providing not just education but a holistic environment conducive to the flourishing of body, soul, and spirit.

4

Helping Young Ladies in Sickness

In assessing the landscape of adolescent health through the lens of mortality rates, there may be a semblance of tranquility. However, a meticulous examination of the well-being of school-aged children unveils a different narrative. Adolescence, marked by rapid growth and transformative developmental changes, is a phase where health disorders proliferate. While not inherently fatal, these disorders significantly compromise the well-being of adolescents, leaving a lasting impact on their future health.

The inherent instability of adolescent health is a natural consequence of the swift pace of growth and the profound physiological transformations occurring during this pivotal period. While the general awareness of the accelerated growth and weight gain in adolescence is widespread, the more intricate and remarkable developmental nuances often escape acknowledgment.

Contrary to childhood, infectious fevers like measles, chickenpox, and whooping cough become less prevalent in adolescence. Yet, a different set of challenges arises, stemming from the stress accompanying rapid development, the organism's struggle to adapt to new functions and conditions, and, to some extent, the lack of wisdom among both adolescents and their advisers.

Delving into specific health concerns, dental issues emerge prominently. A significant number of young individuals seeking enlistment in the army or positions in civil service and missionary societies face rejection due to decayed or defective teeth. Astonishingly, the gravity of this condition often eludes the individuals, their parents, and even medical advisers, despite the potential dangers associated with the condition. Decayed teeth, often accompanied by suppuration around the gums, can lead to severe health implications, including gastric ulcer, appendicitis, heart disease, rheumatoid arthritis, and various local afflictions.

The throat, another focal point, harbors chronic diseases of the tonsils and adenoids, often overlooked until aggravated by external factors. Adenoids, in particular, can disrupt normal bodily functions, leading to mouth breathing, impaired brain function, altered facial appearance, and digestive issues. Timely removal of septic tonsils and adenoids is crucial for restoring health and vitality.

Moving on to digestion, indigestion can be a consequence of swallowing septic materials, but it also has roots in dietary errors and the hurried consumption of food. The preference for unsuitable and indigestible foods, coupled with a rushed morning routine, contributes to indigestion-related illnesses such as anemia and gastric ulcer.

Constipation, often associated with septic processes, underscores the importance of natural bowel movements. Rather than resorting to medications, adopting a diet rich in vegetables, increasing water intake, engaging in regular exercise, and incorporating team games, gymnastics, and dancing into the routine can alleviate constipation.

Headaches, stemming from diverse causes, are frequently linked to undiagnosed vision problems. The reluctance to acknowledge the need for spectacles, fueled by societal misconceptions, can lead to prolonged suffering. In addition, chronic conditions in the nose, mouth, throat, stomach, and bowels can contribute to headaches.

Menstrual abnormalities, a crucial aspect of adolescent health, should occur at regular intervals without pain or distress. However, disruptions caused by over-exertion, unwise activities during menstruation, or exposure to damp or cold conditions can lead to irregularities. The sudden cessation of menstruation can be an early indicator of underlying health issues, warranting prompt medical attention.

A vital aspect of fostering a healthy relationship

with adolescent girls involves open communication about menstruation. Ensuring they understand the correlation between their bodily functions and their future roles as potential mothers can transform initial feelings of shock and humiliation into a sense of modest gladness. Educating girls about the significance of menstruation, its connection to their evolving bodies, and the need for certain restrictions fosters a positive outlook, enabling them to navigate this transformative phase with grace and understanding.

Furthermore, acknowledging the intricate web of factors influencing adolescent health underscores the need for a holistic and proactive approach. An often-neglected aspect is the impact of mental and emotional well-being on physical health during adolescence. The tumultuous journey through puberty, coupled with societal expectations, peer pressures, and academic challenges, can significantly influence mental health. Integrating mental health awareness, support systems, and counseling services into adolescent healthcare can contribute to a more comprehensive and effective well-being strategy.

In the contemporary landscape, technology plays a pivotal role in shaping adolescent lifestyles. The prevalence of screen time, social media exposure, and online activities demands attention when considering overall health. Striking a balance between technological engagement and real-world interactions is essential to prevent potential negative repercussions on both physical and mental health.

Physical activity remains a cornerstone of adolescent health. While traditional team sports and gymnastics are beneficial, diverse forms of exercise, including yoga and recreational activities, should be encouraged to cater to individual preferences. Creating an environment that fosters a positive attitude towards exercise contributes not only to physical fitness but also to mental resilience.

Nutrition, a fundamental aspect of health, needs a modern perspective. Beyond the traditional focus on food groups, considering dietary preferences, cultural influences, and sustainable eating practices becomes crucial. Education on making informed food choices, understanding nutritional labels, and cultivating a healthy relationship with food can empower adolescents to navigate dietary decisions effectively.

Addressing the socio-economic factors influencing adolescent health is equally vital. Disparities in access to healthcare, education, and nutritious food can exacerbate health challenges. Implementing policies that promote inclusivity, affordability, and awareness ensures a more equitable approach to adolescent health.

In conclusion, the multifaceted nature of adolescent health requires a nuanced and contemporary approach. Integrating mental health awareness, leveraging technology responsibly, promoting diverse physical activities, modernizing nutritional education, and addressing socio-economic disparities collectively contribute to a more robust and inclusive healthcare strategy for adolescents. Embracing the evolving landscape of adolescence with proactive and adaptive measures ensures a healthier future generation capable of navigating the complexities of modern life.

5

Mental and Moral Strength

Entering the realm of adolescence in the contemporary era brings forth a plethora of challenges and opportunities. The teenage years, marked by rapid growth and development, are intertwined with the weight of academic expectations. A juxtaposition of societal classes reveals disparities in the educational journey, where the less privileged bid farewell to formal education at the tender age of fourteen. This contrasts sharply with their more affluent counterparts, who, at the same juncture, begin to grasp the significance of education and the purpose it serves.

Education has undergone a transformative evolution in recent years, witnessing a shift towards more intelligent and pupil-centric approaches. The interconnection of diverse subjects has become more evident, fostering a holistic understanding of the educational landscape. However, the system is far from flawless. Special attention must be given, particularly in the case of girls, considering their unique physiological challenges. The adolescent girl undergoes rapid physiological and psychological changes, impacting her ability to consistently engage in strenuous academic pursuits.

Recognizing the ebb and flow of an adolescent girl's capabilities is paramount. There are days when she may not be at her peak performance, requiring a discerning and sympathetic approach from educators. These moments, instead of being wasted, could be utilized for lighter subjects and manual activities that don't demand intense physical exertion. Striking a balance between fostering discipline and allowing flexibility becomes crucial during such times.

Moreover, the curriculum for girls presents

intricate challenges, necessitating resourcefulness, patience, and empathetic insight from educators. Adolescent girls, driven by emulation and a desire for academic excellence, often need protection from themselves. Teaching them the virtues of obedience and a cheerful acceptance of necessary restrictions becomes a vital aspect of their holistic development.

The private school setting introduces its own set of challenges, primarily the need to occupy every waking hour without succumbing to overwork-induced exhaustion. Introducing diverse subjects such as gymnastics, games, dancing, and practical skills like needlework and cooking provides a welcome relief from purely intellectual pursuits.

Transitioning to the realm of elementary schools, where leaving at fourteen is common, the challenges shift but remain significant. The early departure often results in a lack of in-depth assimilation of knowledge acquired, leaving the knowledge base scanty and potentially obsolete in a few years. Bridging the gap between school education and real-world applicability becomes imperative, especially in preparing girls for domestic responsibilities.

The notion of "half-timing" and Continuation Schools for adolescents between fourteen and sixteen raises questions about the effectiveness of the current system. The evenings, which should ideally be reserved for recreation and personal growth, are currently allocated for more study, further contributing to mental fatigue.

As adolescents step into the workforce, the kind of employment available plays a crucial role in shaping their future. Caution must be exercised to steer them away from dead-end occupations, commonly known as "blind alleys." While the richer classes have more opportunities and resources, the need for purposeful engagement remains universal. Whether it's continuing education, pursuing hobbies, or engaging in philanthropy, idle time between school and marriage should be minimized to prevent the cultivation of detrimental habits.

Adolescence, with its myriad challenges and opportunities, necessitates a modern, adaptive approach to education and personal development. Striking a balance between academic rigor, practical skills, and purposeful engagement is key to fostering well-rounded individuals poised for success in the contemporary world.

Amid the complexities of adolescence, a pivotal concern arises in the form of the continuation of education beyond the traditional schooling age. While the concept of Evening Schools exists, its effectiveness is questionable, as the mental fatigue resulting from a full day's work diminishes the potential benefits. Evenings should ideally be dedicated to recreational pursuits, fostering a more balanced and holistic development.

The notion of "half-timing" during regular school hours also presents challenges. It may not be the optimal solution for enhancing the education of adolescents entering the workforce. There is hope that proposed educational reforms, such as Mr. Hayes Fisher's bill, might bring about positive changes and improve the overall educational landscape.

The type of employment available for school-leavers is a critical consideration. Efforts should be directed towards reducing the number of young individuals entering occupations known as "blind alleys," which offer limited prospects for career advancement. This issue is more prevalent among boys, particularly in Scotland, where a significant number end up as messengers. In contrast, girls often have a clearer path, evolving into roles like housemaids, cooks, or shop assistants.

The challenges faced by young people transitioning into the workforce highlight the importance of creating a bridge between formal education and practical skills. The introduction of Technical Schools or Continuation Schools could provide a viable solution, ensuring that adolescents receive the necessary instruction to navigate the complexities of their chosen careers.

However, the implementation of such solutions faces resistance, especially from working-class families reliant on the income brought in by their adolescent children. The tension between immediate financial needs and the long-term benefits of extended education poses a considerable dilemma for families. Balancing the immediate economic contribution of young workers with the long-term advantages of a more educated workforce remains a key challenge.

The significance of purposeful engagement and meaningful employment transcends socio-economic classes. Regardless of their background, adolescents should be encouraged to take up activities that fill their lives with interests and duties. The transition from formal education to adulthood should not be a period of idleness, as it can lead to the cultivation of detrimental habits and a sense of purposelessness.

Parents and guardians play a crucial role in shaping the post-schooling trajectory of their wards. The idea that obligations and duties extend beyond the school or college years is paramount. Even the well-to-do should encourage their daughters to undertake meaningful employment, fostering a sense of responsibility and preventing the pitfalls associated with a lack of purpose.

A crucial point to underscore is that while occupation for the entire day is desirable, excessive hard work should be avoided. Striking a balance that allows for rest and recreation is essential for the physical and mental well-being of adolescents. The optimal duration of work hours varies among individuals, influenced by factors such as the nature of the work and the individual's mental and physical constitution.

In conclusion, navigating the complexities of adolescence requires a nuanced and adaptive approach. Modern education systems need to address the unique challenges faced by adolescents, providing them with a balanced and purposeful trajectory into adulthood. The intersection of education, practical skills, and meaningful engagement is the key to preparing the youth for success in a rapidly evolving world.

6

The Aim of Education

In the contemporary pursuit of preparing the younger generation for their roles as future parents, citizens, and contributors to society, a pressing challenge emerges. The responsibility falls upon educators and guardians to instill in the youth not only high ideals and attractive examples but also to provide the means for adequate preparation. In the current era, our societal landscape is reminiscent of the days of Eli in Israel when the "word of the Lord was scarce." We find ourselves in a civilization marked by surface refinement, a veneer of superficial knowledge, but often lacking enthusiasm and a profound understanding of the true purpose of education and training.

Addressing this unsatisfactory state requires an early intervention, reaching beyond adolescence, even to the cradle. The revival of traditional values like duty, obedience, and discipline must become household principles once again, laying the foundation for a societal renaissance. A poetic voice akin to Browning's logic, Tennyson's sweetness, and Kipling's force is needed to awaken us from our indifference, sloth, and pleasure-seeking tendencies. A national anthem that transcends the superficiality of our current state, propelling us toward the promise that England once held.

Considering the education of girls, it's crucial to reaffirm that the loftiest earthly ideal for a woman is to be a good wife and mother. While this might not need explicit articulation to young girls, their education should naturally guide them toward an intrinsic understanding that wifehood and motherhood represent the pinnacle of their existence. All aspects of learning, skills development, and artistic pursuits should align as preparations for this central goal. Recognizing that each generation is both a product and a seed, educational aims should be subordinate to this overarching purpose.

The primal instinct of fatherhood and motherhood, deeply ingrained in human nature, could serve as a powerful motivator for adolescents. By understanding the sacredness of their bodies and the divine role bestowed upon them, they can strive for the highest degree of personal perfection. However, this noble pursuit is hindered by the prevailing ignorance and reluctance to discuss these matters openly. The conspiracy of silence has led to detrimental consequences, particularly when adolescents, unaware of physiological facts, encounter the realities of life in marriage.

The question of when and how to impart knowledge about reproduction sparks debates. Some advocate for instruction at puberty, others propose a few years later, perhaps on the brink of marriage. There's a growing perspective that treating the facts of reproduction similarly to digestion and respiration, introducing them gradually from early childhood, might be more natural and beneficial. This approach aligns with the understanding that reproduction, though not essential to individual life, is crucial for the life of the nation.

Teaching the facts of physiology to children can begin with a simple acknowledgment of life phenomena around them. Observing the cat with her kittens, the bird with its fledglings, and, most importantly, the mother with her infant, children can grasp the beauty and responsibility of parenthood. Later in adolescence, a more detailed understanding of the father's role in the mystery of reproduction can be introduced, emphasizing the care of one's body and the responsibilities tied to future family life.

An alternative approach involves using the study of vegetable physiology as a gateway to understanding the reproductive process. By illustrating the fertilization of ovules by pollen in plants, analogous concepts in animal physiology can be explained. This method, however, should follow the teaching of domestic animal life to provide a comprehensive understanding for boys and girls.

Parents should recognize that children are naturally curious about the mysteries of life. Whether witnessed in family life, domesticated animals, or literature, the child's thirst for understanding is inherent. Fathers and mothers have the choice to lovingly and reverently unveil these mysteries or allow the child's mind to be tainted by misguided peers and vulgar companions.

In fostering the purity, reverence, and piety of our children, let us strive to keep their honor intact, preserve their innocence, and guide them from the unconscious goodness of childhood to the fully conscious dignity of maturity. The hope is for our sons to grow as young plants and our daughters as the polished corners of the temple, embodying the sublime and beautiful mysteries of life.

To further solidify the holistic education and preparation of the younger generation, we must acknowledge the broader context of our contemporary society. Beyond the ideals of parenthood and family life, today's youth face multifaceted challenges that demand a comprehensive educational approach. It is not merely about cultivating the future fathers and mothers but also about nurturing informed, responsible, and compassionate citizens capable of navigating the complexities of the modern world.

In the quest for a more profound educational paradigm, we encounter the need for a dynamic curriculum that extends beyond traditional boundaries. While emphasizing the significance of family life, it is equally crucial to equip adolescents with skills, knowledge, and values that prepare them for diverse roles in a rapidly evolving society. The call for a poet with the logic of Browning, the sweetness of Tennyson, and the force of Kipling resonates not only in the realm of familial ideals but also in the broader context of societal engagement.

Modern education should embrace interdisciplinary learning, fostering critical thinking, adaptability, and a global perspective. The convergence of technological advancements, cultural diversity, and environmental challenges necessitates an educational framework that transcends narrow boundaries. Young minds must be encouraged to explore, question, and innovate, guided by the ethos of responsible citizenship and a commitment to social justice.

In the context of gender equality, it is paramount to instill in both boys and girls the understanding that their aspirations and capabilities extend beyond traditional gender roles. While recognizing the importance of wifehood and motherhood, girls should also be empowered to pursue careers, leadership roles, and any field of their choice. Boys, in turn, should be taught the principles of equality, respect, and collaboration, fostering a society where all individuals can thrive irrespective of gender.

Addressing the complexities of adolescence requires a nuanced approach that considers the emotional, social, and psychological aspects of development. Open conversations about mental health, self-awareness, and emotional resilience should be integrated into the educational fabric. The aim is to produce individuals who not only excel academically but also possess the emotional intelligence and well-being to navigate the challenges of adulthood.

As we strive for a comprehensive and modern

educational approach, it is essential to recognize the role of technology in shaping the future. Education technology, when leveraged effectively, can enhance learning experiences, promote inclusivity, and prepare students for the digital age. Embracing innovative teaching methods, such as project-based learning, virtual simulations, and collaborative platforms, can foster creativity and problem-solving skills.

In conclusion, the task of preparing the youth for their roles as future parents, citizens, and contributors to society is a multifaceted endeavor. It involves not only instilling high ideals of parenthood but also equipping them with the skills, knowledge, and values needed to thrive in a complex and interconnected world. A modern education must be dynamic, interdisciplinary, and inclusive, fostering a generation capable of embracing diversity, driving positive change, and contributing to the collective well-being of humanity.

7

Now for the Young Men

In the upcoming sections of this guide, the term "puberty" will be frequently referenced. To ensure clarity, let's start with a concise overview of puberty's phenomena. Puberty designates the age when a boy becomes capable of fatherhood. In temperate climates, this typically occurs around fifteen, though it can vary, with some reaching this stage as early as twelve and others as late as seventeen. An unmistakable sign of puberty is the changing pitch of the voice, transitioning from awkward squeaks to a more mature, bass tone.

This phase is pivotal, marking significant changes in both the body and the mind. The reproductive organs undergo substantial development, becoming responsive to various stimuli—be they physical or mental. The testicles start producing seminal fluid, now containing spermatazoa, crucial for reproduction. Sexual thoughts trigger the secretion of this fluid, often resulting in involuntary nocturnal emissions. While some view these emissions as normal, there is room for skepticism based on personal observations.

Another physical transformation linked to puberty involves the growth of hair in the pubic area and on the face, with the latter exhibiting a slower progression. Alongside the newfound ability for fatherhood, a potent surge in the sexual instinct occurs, manifesting as passion and lust—a blend of unconscious and conscious sexual desire. This passion sometimes leads to an exaggerated susceptibility to female attractions, often unnoticed in its sexual nature. In those with sexual knowledge, there's a tendency to dwell on sexual thoughts, especially when the mind is idle. While passion and lust don't instantly reach their full strength, their arrival during a period of weakened self-control, coupled with the allure of novelty, can dominate the mind even in normative cases, potentially becoming tyrannous if the reproductive system is prematurely stimulated.

Attaining puberty frequently coincides with heightened self-consciousness and an antagonistic stance toward authority figures. However, it's crucial to challenge the common belief that puberty directly causes these shifts. Self-consciousness, when present in boyhood, typically results from an unclean inner life, with puberty merely intensifying its effects. In contrast, a clean mind experiences minimal change in this aspect during puberty. The observed antagonism towards authority can be attributed to external influences, as puberty amplifies the desire to fit in and project a sense of manliness. Unfortunately, a distorted public opinion may demand a superficial version of manliness—embracing profanity, tobacco, and irreverence—suppressing any inclination towards higher ideals. Conversely, a healthy public opinion, aligning with a boy's nobler instincts, encourages a dedication to lofty ideals and prompts the use of newfound energies for personal development and addressing societal wrongs during this transformative period of puberty.

As adolescents navigate through the tumultuous waters of puberty, it becomes increasingly evident that this stage is not solely a physical metamorphosis but a profound psychological and emotional journey. The turbulence of these changes is further exemplified by the surge in self-consciousness and the perceived rebellion against authority, aspects often misunderstood as inherent consequences of puberty.

Self-consciousness during adolescence is not an inherent byproduct of physical maturation. Instead, it is often rooted in the complexities of an individual's inner life. A clean and healthy mental landscape tends to experience minimal disruption in self-consciousness during puberty. However, when coupled with unresolved psychological issues or an unclean inner life, puberty has the potential to magnify existing self-consciousness, creating a more challenging terrain for adolescents to navigate.

Similarly, the seemingly rebellious attitude towards authority figures that frequently emerges during puberty is not an inevitable outcome of hormonal changes. Rather, it is profoundly influenced by external factors, particularly societal expectations and peer pressures. The desire to fit in, be perceived as manly, or adhere to a distorted notion of maturity can lead adolescents to adopt behaviors and attitudes that defy conventional authority.

Understanding these nuances is crucial for parents, educators, and society at large. Instead of attributing every shift in behavior solely to puberty, a more nuanced approach involves recognizing the intricate interplay between internal and external influences. Creating an environment that fosters open communication, empathy, and a healthy understanding of self and others is paramount during this critical phase.

Moreover, the prevailing narrative around adolescence should shift from one of apprehension and concern to a more positive and empowering perspective. Adolescents, armed with the right guidance and support, have the potential to channel the energy and newfound abilities of puberty into positive endeavors. A robust public opinion, aligned with virtuous ideals, can inspire adolescents to pursue excellence, challenge societal wrongs, and contribute meaningfully to their communities.

In the chapters that follow, we will delve deeper into the multifaceted aspects of puberty, offering insights, guidance, and a more holistic understanding of this transformative phase in a young person's life. By embracing the complexities and challenges of adolescence, we can collectively nurture a generation that not only survives puberty but emerges from it with resilience, wisdom, and a strong sense of purpose.

8

∾

The Struggle for Young Boys to Be Good Men

In the realm of challenges confronting the maturing young lad, all are acknowledged and, to some extent, addressed—save for the most inevitable and perilous threat of all. Concerning the use and potential misuse of reproductive organs, the majority of boys have, until now, navigated these murky waters devoid of mature guidance. Instead, they have formed their perceptions from less refined companions and incidental references in sources like the Bible and other texts. Under these circumstances, only a scant few boys manage to evade two particularly menacing pitfalls: the artificial stimulation of reproductive organs and the absorption of debased notions surrounding sexuality.

The ramifications of this lack of guidance extend beyond premature curtailment of life and the permanent enfeeblement of constitutions. Numerous lads, who might have otherwise confronted the sexual challenges of adulthood successfully, capitulate to them almost effortlessly, revealing the insidious nature of the perils concealed within the inner lives of boys and men.

Between the two evils, self-abuse, while still yielding manifold and disastrous consequences, is deemed the lesser transgression. Some boys outgrow the physical injuries inflicted upon themselves in their uninformed youth. Yet, fewer can entirely cleanse their minds from the impure desires entwined with their understanding of sex. These desires render young men impotent in the face of temptation, leading even those of kind disposition to inflict agony, misery, and degradation upon innocent girls through seduction. The most degrading vices are pursued with prostitutes on the street, and the atmosphere of social life is tainted with filthy talk and ribald jests. Even a pure and ennobling passion struggles to redeem them, as the pure stream of human love becomes turbid with lust. The temporary upliftment in marriage is overshadowed by broken vows, transforming the blessings of home life into wormwood and gall.

The endurance of a system so destructive to physical and spiritual health until now will likely soon become a source of widespread astonishment. The evidence highlighting the prevalence of youthful perversion in recent years challenges the unreasonable assumptions that have propped up this system. In subsequent chapters, we will delve into the conclusions drawn by teachers with direct experience in these matters.

Various teachers, whose authority in most matters far exceeds my own, might find it presumptuous to present my experiences first. However, I dare to do so because, as far as I am aware, no other teacher has offered such explicit evidence. The paper I presented in 1908 at the London University before the International Congress on Moral Education has gained recognition, being considered of great significance by competent judges. Its subsequent republication in the Headquarters Gazette, the official organ of the Boy Scout movement, adds weight to its importance.

At that time, presenting my results to the public required courage, as I was unaware that eminent figures in the educational world had already made sweeping, if less precise, statements. Emboldened by this revelation and the commendations received, I now quote a significant portion of that paper, anticipating that it will provide context for the more general statements made by distinguished individuals such as Canon Lyttelton, Mr. A.C. Benson, and Dr. Clement Dukes.

This brings me to an important point—my credentials. I emphasize them to establish the character and limitations of my experience. In a world where confident generalizations often arise from limited or nonexistent experience, particularly in the realm of education and discussions on sensitive subjects, it is crucial to present one's credentials before addressing the public.

The narrative now shifts to a series of cases derived from personal experience, aiming to illustrate the prevalence and consequences of sexual issues among boys. Each case serves as a poignant example, shedding light on the blind spots of parents, the misleading notion that natural refinement provides sufficient protection, and the misconception that the consequences of secret sins are enough to deter young boys from engaging in harmful behavior.

These cases, ranging from corruption learned in a country village to the consequences of bullying at school, serve as glimpses into the complex world of adolescent sexuality, dispelling myths and underscoring the urgency of addressing these issues with candor and guidance.

Now, let me shed light on the reader about the fact that the conclusions I've drawn regarding the awareness of sexual knowledge among boys and the prevalence of self-abuse are strongly supported by the insights of esteemed educators and medical professionals. Canon Lyttelton, a figure of unquestionable authority, shares his wisdom gleaned from years of experience. Having been educated at Eton, served as an assistant master at Wellington College, headed Haileybury College for fifteen years, and currently holding the position of headmaster at Eton for over six years, his intimate knowledge of boys is profound.

Canon Lyttelton, in his work "Training of the Young in Laws of Sex," doesn't find it necessary to emphasize the prevalence of impurity among boys, as he considers it obvious and, unfortunately, inevitable under current conditions. Quoting him, "In the public school, owing not only to freer talk and more mixed company but to the boy's own wider range of vision, sexual questions, and also those connected with the structure of the body, come to the fore." He expresses concern that, in facing the challenges of adolescence, boys often navigate through a difficult terrain without adequate guidance.

Now, let's turn to the insights of Mr. A.C. Benson, a distinguished modern teacher, known for his extended experience in both public-school life as a student and a master. He addresses the uncomfortable reality that many teachers shy away from discussing such topics, fearing they might introduce inappropriate ideas into boys' minds. Benson asserts, "The standard of purity is low: a vicious boy does not find his vicious tendencies by any means a bar to social success." His observations highlight the challenges of maintaining innocence in the environment of a public school.

Dr. Clement Dukes, the eminent medical officer of Rugby School and an authority on school hygiene, adds his perspective. According to him, widespread ignorance among boys about the consequences of self-abuse is a significant factor contributing to its prevalence, estimating it to be as high as 90 to 95 percent in boarding schools. Professor Stanley Hall, in his comprehensive work on Adolescence, reinforces these concerns, stating that research consistently reveals appalling rates of prevalence.

In conclusion, it's essential to avoid misconceptions that these opinions are specific only to the conditions at Haileybury, Eton, and Rugby. Instead, they mirror the prevalent conditions across numerous schools, reflecting the almost universal state of boys' schools. The urgent need for awareness and education on these matters cannot be overstated, emphasizing the critical role educators play in shaping the well-being of the younger generation.

9

~

Why Do Boys Become That Kind of Man?

The evidence I presented in the previous chapters should convince most readers that maintaining innocence among boys beyond their school age is a rare phenomenon. However, there might be a few who struggle to reconcile this conclusion with their perceptions of boyhood. Let's now explore current beliefs on this topic and reveal their fundamental inaccuracies.

Some people believe that a boy's innate modesty

is sufficient protection against impurity. Does real-life experience support such a notion? Those familiar with children understand that even fundamental virtues like truthfulness and honesty often need to be learned. Ideas of personal cleanliness, self-restraint regarding food, and consideration for others are typically instilled and nurtured. While some children quickly grasp these virtues, many take time, and by the age of ten or twelve, a lively young lad may not be meticulously clean in various aspects.

It's evident that cleanliness and virtue are acquired traits, not innate qualities. Children growing up among unprincipled individuals often adopt similar traits. If a child from a refined background were left without guidance on table manners and morals, relying solely on examples from less refined influences, expecting refinement and consideration would be unrealistic. This analogy extends to the topic of personal purity, where children lack good examples, precepts, and awareness.

In such conditions, expecting a boy to grow up pure is akin to expecting him to grow up greedy. Puberty introduces a potent appetite, heightened by stimulating environmental factors. The act that satisfies this appetite is pleasurable, and the boy, accustomed to certain self-soothing habits, doesn't perceive the harm. The absence of guidance, combined with the indulgent nature of the pleasure, leads to inevitable challenges.

What's remarkable is how earnestly a boy endeavors to cleanse his life once he understands the gravity of his actions. Mistakes are often rooted in ignorance and thoughtlessness, not moral perversity. Harsh rebukes and punishments are seldom just or effective. Instances of rebellion against authority after puberty are usually traced back to inadequate training at home or school. Boys with a solid foundation in both aspects typically adapt positively to healthy public opinion.

Some might assume that adults' reticence about reproduction would naturally discourage a child from playing with private parts or discussing their functions with peers. However, this assumption overlooks a psychological error. The child, accustomed to avoiding public references to bodily needs, doesn't equate this reticence with private acts. This

misjudgment extends to conversations about reproduction, with a corrupt boy's manner making these
discussions seem secretive and unclean.

While many believe that impure thoughts must
manifest in overt acts, this is not always the case.
Knowledge on these subjects is often gained under
conditions of utmost secrecy, reinforced by the behavior of adults. The habit of self-abuse typically
occurs in private, further complicating detection.

It might seem inconceivable that a boy can harbor impure feelings without obvious deterioration,
but human nature challenges this assumption. Even
spiritual individuals may grapple with thoughts
they find shameful. Adults' inconsistency is well-
recognized, and children, being even more obvious
in their inconsistencies, demonstrate a robust ability
to maintain overall soul health despite local morbid
conditions.

Impurity, likened to a disease, has a prolonged
incubation period, often occurring without the
victim's awareness. Its slow development means vis-
ible symptoms might take a long time to appear,

allowing corruption to set in and potentially ruin the entire life.

The insidious nature of impurity as a metaphorical disease with a prolonged incubation period underscores the challenges in detecting its presence. When contracted, its effects may remain hidden for an extended duration, and the individual might remain oblivious to the imminent danger. The internal nature of this "disease" and its slow progression mean that apparent symptoms might not surface until much later.

In the interim, a subtle corruption may silently infiltrate various aspects of the individual's life, potentially wreaking havoc on their overall well-being. This underscores the importance of addressing the issue proactively and providing guidance to young minds, as the ramifications might not become evident until much later.

It's crucial to recognize that a child's journey toward understanding personal purity is a process influenced by both nature and nurture. While innate tendencies play a role, the environment, guidance, and societal expectations significantly shape the outcome. Therefore, it becomes imperative for adults, caregivers, and educators to navigate this delicate terrain with sensitivity, fostering an atmosphere of open communication and providing the necessary tools for informed decision-making.

The outdated notion that a boy's innate modesty alone is sufficient to guard against impurity fails to acknowledge the complexities of human development and the impact of societal influences. Instead, a more nuanced approach that considers the interplay of innate tendencies and learned behaviors is essential.

In conclusion, the exploration of this topic necessitates a shift from outdated beliefs to a modern understanding that aligns with the complexities of human psychology, the impact of societal factors, and the developmental stages of individuals. This shift is not only crucial for fostering healthy attitudes toward personal purity but also for cultivating an environment where young minds can navigate the challenges of adolescence with knowledge, resilience, and a sense of responsibility.

10

∽

What Boys Become

It is challenging to overstate the harmful consequences arising from the current system in which
boys mature into adulthood without proper guidance on matters of sex. As previously mentioned, the
immediate physical repercussions of self-abuse are
relatively minor when compared to the corruption
of the mind resulting from distorted sexual ideas.
Nevertheless, these physical effects are not negligible
and, in some cases, can be quite serious. The widespread prevalence of self-abuse among boys, coupled with the inherent uncertainty regarding a boy's
engagement in this behavior, complicates efforts to

establish a reliable comparison between those practicing chastity and those engaging in self-abuse.

A more meaningful comparison emerges when assessing individual cases, considering a boy's condition during periods of self-indulgence in masturbation and contrasting it with his state after abandoning or significantly reducing the habit. It's unequivocal that a marked difference in a boy's vitality and spiritual well-being follows the relinquishment of this habit.

In the pamphlet, "Private Knowledge for Boys," a poignant passage from Acton on the Reproductive Organs is quoted, providing insight into the contrast between continent and incontinent boys. However, it's crucial to note that specialists like Dr. Acton, focused on male reproductive organ diseases, primarily encounter extreme and abnormal cases, influencing their overall perspective. While Acton's work is recommended for those seeking a comprehensive examination of sex diseases from a specialist with high moral intent, my own estimation, as detailed in the referenced pamphlet, expands on these views.

Dr. Acton's portrayal pertains to extreme cases, prompting me to express, "You will notice that Dr. Acton is here describing an extreme case. I want to tell you what the results are in a case that is not extreme." The pamphlet delves into the various outcomes, emphasizing that the extent of injury varies based on a boy's constitution, the frequency of indulgence, and individual predispositions. The injuries manifest as loss of will-power, self-reliance, shyness, nervousness, irritability, failure of reasoning powers and memory, laziness of body and mind, a diseased fondness for girls, and deceitfulness.

Dr. Clement Dukes, with broad and normal experience, provides a perspective of immense importance. Summing up his opinion, he emphasizes the moral, intellectual, and physical harm resulting from self-abuse. Physically, it acts as a frequent drain during a critical phase of life, impacting growth and development. It inflicts a powerful nervous shock on a system ill-prepared to handle it, leading to muscular and mental debility, loss of spirit and manliness, and potential occurrences of insanity, suicide, and homicide. Beyond the physical, self-abuse induces lethargy, obtuseness, incapacity for mental work, and most significantly, it stains the entire character and undermines life.

This discussion, jointly addressing perverted sex knowledge and self-abuse as impurity, sheds light on the earliest evil stemming from impurity—the deterioration of the intimacy between the boy and his parents. This deterioration is accompanied by a life of duplicity, concealing an inner world from those who were once spiritual guides. The consequences extend to various aspects of the boy's character, and this division between home influences significantly impacts his moral being.

Impurity also instills a self-centered perspective in the boy's approach to sexual relations. While other aspects of life are influenced by multiple motives—such as the desire to please, excel, fulfill duty, or seek truth—the sexual appetite becomes exclusively focused on personal enjoyment. This limited perspective has deplorable consequences, as discussed in the next chapter.

The coarse discussions surrounding sexual relations, often found in impure environments, lead to a loss of reverence. Sacred elements, which should be approached with awe and respect, lose their inspiration when subjected to jest and mockery. The degradation of these sacred aspects contributes to the decline of the soul's light and the lowering of humanity to a bestial level.

The negative effects of impurity extend to a young man's ability to face the sexual temptations of manhood. Many, despite being admirable in other aspects of life, succumb to the vices of prostitution or the less demoralizing but cruel sin of seduction. The societal consequences are dire, with the prevalence of ruined lives and the pervasiveness of death and corruption.

Dr. Dukes emphasizes the root of prostitution and similar vices lies in the impurity of boyhood. Addressing this issue requires a focus on making young boys purer, thereby reducing the demand for and supply of prostitution. Teaching chastity is not only a means of decreasing the demand for prostitutes but also diminishes the supply. Most girls turn to the streets after being seduced, and the antecedents of seduction are rooted in the morbid exaggeration of the sexual appetite and the lack of self-control fostered by youthful impurity.

The selfishness bred by impurity manifests early, with boys displaying callousness towards the cruelty associated with sexual assault. The blind and indifferent nature of impurity leads some young men, who are otherwise refined and generous, to subject innocent girls to torturous consequences. The consequences of seduction are particularly severe, often resulting in a girl's descent into prostitution.

Young men are sometimes ignorant of the fact that sexual relations with prostitutes frequently lead to foul and terrible diseases. Venereal diseases, initiating in the private parts but spreading to other areas of the body, wreak havoc on the general health of those affected. This health risk is not a private concern but impacts the individual's ability to contribute to society and places an unjust burden on family members, particularly a spouse and children.

The blessings of home and monogamy are overshadowed by a societal condition that offers young men limited alternatives to chastity. As economic pressures delay marriage, and the rising standard of living makes it a luxury for many, the urgency of addressing social purity becomes increasingly apparent. Instructing the young in matters of sex stands out as the most crucial social reform, holding the potential to liberate future generations from the pervasive corruption and misery inflicted by lust.

The burden placed on young men today, stemming from ignorance in their formative years, leads to the domination of passions and the enslavement of the will. Even if they enter into marriage, the neglected sex education makes them more susceptible to physical attractions than qualities that contribute to a successful marriage. This susceptibility often results in transient benefits from marriage, as both partners become susceptible to other attachments, reigniting the struggles associated with impurity.

Should the young men of today succumb to the pitfalls of impurity, they grapple with a burden that exceeds the capacity of most ordinary individuals. Ignorance during their formative years renders their boyhood and youth prey to lust, empowering their passions to become tyrannical forces that enslave the will. Even if these individuals enter into the institution of marriage, their troubles persist. As animals, men are neither inherently monogamous nor wholly constant, and the lack of comprehensive sex education exacerbates this tendency.

The inadequacy of sex education makes these individuals more susceptible to physical attractions than to the qualities that make a spouse a good companion, housekeeper, and mother. Consequently, the beneficial influence of marriage becomes ephemeral, and the domestic atmosphere loses its congeniality. Both husband and wife become prone to developing attachments elsewhere, reigniting the age-old struggle associated with impurity.

To illustrate the gravity of these consequences, consider a hypothetical scenario: If children were to harbor an instinctive and escalating desire for alcohol from infancy, with secret and unchecked means to satisfy this craving, the nation would find itself inhabited by individuals who, due to ignorance, become slaves to the vice of alcohol. Society would be populated by individuals willing to break any law

—human or divine—that impedes the gratification of this overpowering need. Such a society would be comprised of men and women intoxicated by this vice, ready to disregard all moral and legal constraints in the pursuit of their insatiable desires.

The burdens placed upon today's young men are immense, creating a vicious cycle of lust, enslavement, and societal struggles. The call for a transformation in societal attitudes and a comprehensive approach to sex education becomes increasingly urgent. The aim is not just to mitigate the consequences but to prevent the very roots of these issues.

In conclusion, the societal impact of impurity extends far beyond individual lives. It affects families, communities, and the nation at large. The need for a robust and morally grounded sex education system is paramount. By instilling values of purity, responsibility, and reverence, we can empower the younger generation to break free from the shackles of impurity and contribute to the creation of a society marked by healthier relationships, stronger families, and a more harmonious coexistence. The time to act is now, recognizing that the well-being of our society hinges on the enlightenment and empowerment of its future custodians.

11

 ～

Knowledge Protects Innocence

For those who've been with me on this journey through the earlier chapters, I trust you sense that despite any reservations about providing explicit sex education to the young, it's far superior to the almost inevitable distortions that arise from ignorance. If we had to pick between a state of "innocence" and one of informed knowledge approached with reverence, some might lean towards the former. However, that's not a real choice. It boils down to leaving a young person to glean information from crude and unsavory sources or delivering it ourselves in a way that imbues it from the start with sacredness and dignity.

Even if you're still inclined to view sex education as, at best, a somewhat taboo secret, you'd likely agree that it could be communicated with less harm by a caring adult than by vulgar and irreverent voices.

I won't leave you stranded in this dilemma. I firmly believe in the wisdom shared by Canon Lyttelton, whose words stem from profound spiritual insight: "To a lover of nature, no less than to a convinced Christian, the subject ought to wear an aspect not only negatively innocent but positively beautiful." It's a recurring miracle, an embodiment of law, and a topic that can be embraced with purity. A normally-constituted child's mind, when presented with the right perspective, can absorb this subject positively from the start.

The present system's shortcomings are evident in the prevailing beliefs on this matter. Currently, sexual knowledge is often acquired from less-than-reputable sources, and no amount of purification can entirely free it from its original associations with uncleanness.

Some see the marriage certificate as a license for impurity, and sexual union as an animal indulgence nearly impossible to resist. This outlook, however, stands in stark contrast to the ideal that love is a virtue for heroes, pure as snow on high hills, and immortal as every great soul that struggles, endures, and fulfills.

The challenge is to break away from these antiquated ideas that continue to perpetuate a flawed system. It's essential to challenge preconceptions and advocate for a more enlightened perspective. Those who aspire to uplift humanity must find the courage to speak out, even when faced with accusations of indecency.

This is not the ideal space to delve deeply into such a delicate matter, but we can't completely sidestep it here. So, let me offer a few suggestions.

Firstly, can we genuinely believe that the most noble and spiritual individuals would compromise their integrity in the eyes of the one they love most?

Would they engage in an indelicate act that would tarnish the sanctity of their relationship? A great poet, who remained an ardent lover until his wife's last moments, beautifully captured the essence of love and its ability to elevate human qualities.

Moreover, as believers in a divine order, can we accept that the perpetuation of the race hinges on acts of sin or indelicacy? Is God endorsing a ceremony that leads to sin? Is the God we address as "Our Father" willing to be associated with a name that inherently connects to impurity? Has He, in the strongest of our instincts, embedded something that cannot elevate but must debase?

Lastly, our bodies serve as instruments for expressing emotions, and bodily contact is the most obvious way to express affection. The most intimate embraces, in the context of marriage, should not be seen merely as physical pleasure but as a means of expressing profound emotion. Failure to understand this often leads to the breakdown of happiness in many marriages.

In conclusion, arguments suggesting that sexual

union is purely physical and should be regarded as such miss the mark. Our understanding of physical acts, such as eating and drinking, has evolved beyond mere animal behavior. Similarly, we should elevate our perspective on sexual union, viewing it not only as a physical act but also as a profound expression of emotions and connection. The idea is to move beyond outdated views and cultivate a healthier, more enlightened perspective on this fundamental aspect of human life.

෧

Teaching Our Young Men

For those who've been with me on this journey through the earlier chapters, I trust you sense that despite any reservations about providing explicit sex education to the young, it's far superior to the almost inevitable distortions that arise from ignorance. If we had to pick between a state of "innocence" and one of informed knowledge approached with reverence, some might lean towards the former. However, that's not a real choice. It boils down to leaving a young person to glean information from crude and unsavory sources or delivering it ourselves in a way that imbues it from the start with sacredness and dignity.

Even if you're still inclined to view sex education as, at best, a somewhat taboo secret, you'd likely agree that it could be communicated with less harm by a caring adult than by vulgar and irreverent voices.

I won't leave you stranded in this dilemma. I firmly believe in the wisdom shared by Canon Lyttelton, whose words stem from profound spiritual insight: "To a lover of nature, no less than to a convinced Christian, the subject ought to wear an aspect not only negatively innocent but positively beautiful." It's a recurring miracle, an embodiment of law, and a topic that can be embraced with purity. A normally-constituted child's mind, when presented with the right perspective, can absorb this subject positively from the start.

The present system's shortcomings are evident in the prevailing beliefs on this matter. Currently, sexual knowledge is often acquired from less-than-reputable sources, and no amount of purification can entirely free it from its original associations with uncleanness.

Some see the marriage certificate as a license for impurity, and sexual union as an animal indulgence nearly impossible to resist. This outlook, however, stands in stark contrast to the ideal that love is a virtue for heroes, pure as snow on high hills, and immortal as every great soul that struggles, endures, and fulfills.

The challenge is to break away from these antiquated ideas that continue to perpetuate a flawed system. It's essential to challenge preconceptions and advocate for a more enlightened perspective. Those who aspire to uplift humanity must find the courage to speak out, even when faced with accusations of indecency.

This is not the ideal space to delve deeply into such a delicate matter, but we can't completely sidestep it here. So, let me offer a few suggestions.

Firstly, can we genuinely believe that the most noble and spiritual individuals would compromise their integrity in the eyes of the one they love most?

Would they engage in an indelicate act that would tarnish the sanctity of their relationship? A great poet, who remained an ardent lover until his wife's last moments, beautifully captured the essence of love and its ability to elevate human qualities.

Moreover, as believers in a divine order, can we accept that the perpetuation of the race hinges on acts of sin or indelicacy? Is God endorsing a ceremony that leads to sin? Is the God we address as "Our Father" willing to be associated with a name that inherently connects to impurity? Has He, in the strongest of our instincts, embedded something that cannot elevate but must debase?

Lastly, our bodies serve as instruments for expressing emotions, and bodily contact is the most obvious way to express affection. The most intimate embraces, in the context of marriage, should not be seen merely as physical pleasure but as a means of expressing profound emotion. Failure to understand this often leads to the breakdown of happiness in many marriages.

Arguments suggesting that sexual union is

purely physical and should be regarded as such miss the mark. Our understanding of physical acts, such as eating and drinking, has evolved beyond mere animal behavior. Similarly, we should elevate our perspective on sexual union, viewing it not only as a physical act but also as a profound expression of emotions and connection. The idea is to move beyond outdated views and cultivate a healthier, more enlightened perspective on this fundamental aspect of human life.

To truly grasp the significance of this shift in perspective, consider the progression in our understanding of basic acts like eating and drinking. In primitive times, these activities were purely animalistic. Yet, as societies developed, we transformed meals into social rituals, sometimes even elevating them to a sacramental level in religious practices.

Sexual union, like eating and drinking, shouldn't be confined to its physical aspect alone. It's time to recognize its deeper dimensions—expressions of profound emotions, spiritual connection, and the unity of two individuals. The contention that this is too transcendental a view misses the mark. Just as we've redefined our relationship with food and drink, we must do the same with our understanding of sexual intimacy.

The prevailing notion that sex is primarily physical has led to misguided pursuits of sexual excitement and the perception of intercourse as a mere act of pleasure. This mindset often arises from the absence of proper guidance during a young person's formative years. The natural, yet misguided, craving for sexual excitement grows in the absence of wise counsel, jeopardizing the foundations of many marriages.

Furthermore, let's challenge the assumption that the chaste and spiritual must be separate from the physical. The passion between lovers, though indisputably sexual, can encompass the highest ideals of thought, amiable words, courtliness, a desire for fame, and a love of truth—the very qualities that make us human.

Our bodies serve as vehicles for expressing a range of emotions, from the innocent caresses of childhood to the most intimate expressions of love.

The spontaneity and unrestrained nature of these gestures, often lost as we grow older, find their culmination in the sacred embrace of lovers. It's crucial to comprehend that these expressions, while undoubtedly pleasurable, are sought not for the sake of physical pleasure but as a means of conveying deep-seated emotions.

An enlightened perspective on sexual matters doesn't discount the physical aspect but places it within the broader context of emotional expression and spiritual connection. Sex education, when approached with reverence and openness, is not met with shame but rather received with instant reverence by those whose minds have not been tainted.

Canon Lyttelton eloquently captures the innocence and readiness of little children to understand the profound mysteries of life when presented with truthfulness, understanding, and guileless delicacy. The beauty of children's innocence lies not in shielding them from the truth but in guiding them through the revelation of the deep harmonies of nature's laws.

In conclusion, the need for a paradigm shift in our understanding of sexual matters is evident. By challenging outdated beliefs and embracing a more enlightened perspective, we can ensure that sex education is not stigmatized but rather seen as a sacred and essential aspect of human experience. The task requires courage and a willingness to confront societal norms, but the potential for positive change in individual lives and the broader culture is immense.